Our Families

Grandfathers
Are Part of a Family

by Lucia Raatma

CAPSTONE PRESS
a capstone imprint

Little Pebble is published by Capstone Press,
1710 Roe Crest Drive, North Mankato, Minnesota 56003
www.mycapstone.com

**Library of Congress Cataloging-in-Publication Data is available
on the Library of Congress website**

ISBN: 978-1-5157-7458-7 (library binding)
ISBN: 978-1-5157-7469-3 (paperback)
written by Lucia Raatma

Editorial Credits
Christianne Jones, editor; Juliette Peters, designer;
Wanda Winch, media researcher; Laura Manthe, production specialist

Photo Credits
Capstone Studio: Karon Dubke, 5, 7, 13, 15, 19, 21; Shutterstock: Angelina Babii, paper
texture, Burlingham, 9, Diego Cervo, 1, Dragon Images, cover, Monkey Business Images, 11,
Teguh Mujiono, tree design; Thinkstock: Photodisc, 17

Table of Contents

Grandfathers

A grandfather is the father
of your mother or father.
He can be called grandpa.

A grandpa may have grandsons. He may also have granddaughters.

What Grandfathers Do

Wilson's grandpa goes to work. He is a teacher.

Jack's grandpa lives near Jack. They like to fish.

Jacy's grandpa is a farmer.

He works hard.

Jada lives with her grandpa.

They like to play and laugh.

Brad's grandpa lives far away. They talk on the phone.

Teddy likes to ride
his bike. His grandpa
helps him.

Grandpas help.

They love.

They hug.

Glossary

granddaughter—a female child of one's son or daughter

grandfather—the father of a mother or father

grandson—a male child of one's son or daughter

Read More

Ajmera, Maya. *Our Grandparents: A Global Album.* Watertown, MA: Charlesbridge, 2010.

Harris, Robie H. *Who's in My Family?* All About Our Families. Somerville, MA: Candlewick, 2012.

Hunter, Nick. *Finding Out About Your Family History.* Mankato, MN: Heinemann-Raintree, 2015.

Internet Sites

FactHound offers a safe, fun way to find Internet sites related to this book. All of the sites on FactHound have been researched by our staff.

Here's all you do:
Visit *www.facthound.com*
Type in this code: 9781515774587

Check out projects, games and lots more at
www.capstonekids.com

Index